FIDGET SPINNER

TRICKS, HACKS & MODS

FIDGET SPINNER

TRICKS, HACKS & MODS

AMAZE YOUR FRIENDS WITH SPECTACULAR SPINNER SECRETS!

CARA STEVENS

PHOTOGRAPHS BY JASON GROW

FOR YOUNG READERS

RACEHORSE FOR YOUNG READERS

Racehorse for Young Readers™ books may be purchased in bulk at special discounts for sales promotion, corporate gifts, fund-raising, or educational purposes. Special editions can also be created to specifications. For details, contact the Special Sales Department, Racehorse for Young Readers, 307 West 36th Street, 11th Floor, New York, NY 10018 or info@skyhorsepublishing.com.

Racehorse for Young Readers™ is a pending trademark of Skyhorse Publishing, Inc.®, a Delaware corporation.

Visit our website at www.skyhorsepublishing.com.

10 9 8 7 6 5 4 3 2 1

Library of Congress Cataloging-in-Publication Data is available on file.

Cover photographs: Shutterstock.com
Cover design by Michael Short

Interior photographs by Jason Grow, Allan Penn, and Shutterstock.com
Interior design and production by Nick Grant

Hardcover ISBN: 978-1-63158-248-6
Ebook ISBN: 978-1-63158-249-3

Printed in the United States of America

Acknowledgements
Special thanks go out to the fantastic fidget spinner models:
Lucy Bartlett, Max Kirk, Ben Mark, Lily Mark, and Owen Schmidt.

This book wouldn't be the same without your
smiling faces and fidget skills!

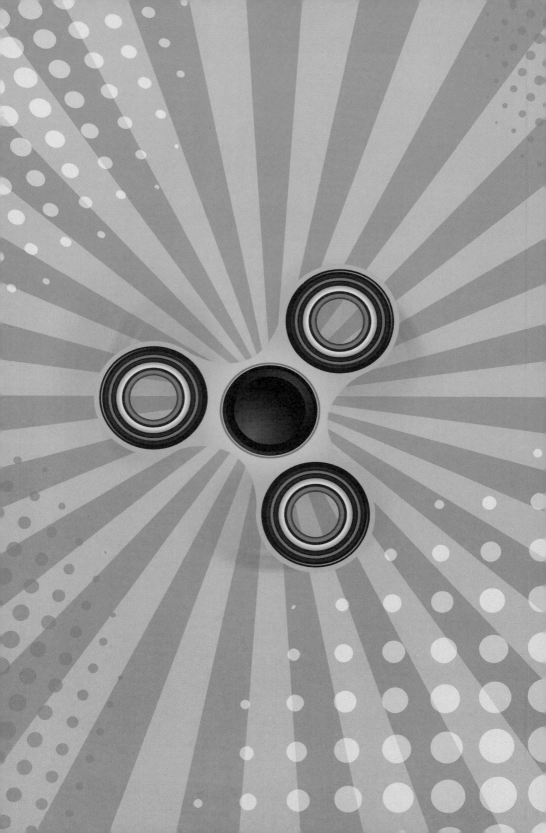

TABLE OF CONTENTS

CHAPTER ONE: WHAT IS FIDGET SPINNING?

A fidget spinner is a small toy that fits in the palm of your hand. The center is a ball bearing and it's surrounded by perfectly weighted spokes or prongs. At the most basic level, you flick the spokes to spin the spinner. But if that were all there were to it, the fun would end before it even began.

What's the big deal about spinners?

With a fidget spinner, the whole is more than the sum of its parts. Taken individually, the frame, bearing, spokes, weights, and buttons are no big deal. But put them together and you get one of the coolest toys out there and one that'll guarantee hours of fun.

What you can do with a fidget spinner

- Spin it
- Time it
- Learn cool tricks
- Compete for records
- Play games against friends
- Fight boredom
- Capture your feats on video
- Show off your tricks
- Or just spin a spinner, sit back, relax, and zone out.

What a fidget spinner is good for

- **Blasting away boredom:** This pocket-sized fidget tool can keep your idle hands and brain busy for hours on end, whether you're stuck in the back seat on a long car ride, standing in the cafeteria line, or waiting for your parents to pick you up.

- **Amping up your reflexes:** Practice makes perfect, and mastering fidget spinner tricks doesn't just make you the next big YouTube star or the master of recess. It also helps your brain build new connections. Whether you're kind of clumsy or just need to improve your hand-eye coordination for sports, keep practicing and you should see a difference.

- **Boosting creativity:** Obsessed with tricking out your fidget spinner and trying new tricks? You aren't wasting time—you're giving your creative brain a healthy workout!

- **Getting science-y with spinner physics:** What makes the spinner work? How can you make it spin faster? Where do you need to hold your hand to catch the spinner at the exact time and place? You may not realize it, but when you think about the mechanics of your spinner, you're actually piecing together one of the greatest mysteries of our universe.

- **Fidgeting, fiddling, and fun:** If you're like many people and you absently take apart pens and put them back together, unbend paper clips, pick at the carpet or your hair, or idly fiddle with whatever is nearby, a fidget spinner can quietly focus your energy in a less destructive way.

- **Making you Internet-famous, maybe:** With practice, you can get pretty good at fidget spinner tricks in a very short time. Once you've mastered some totally rad tricks, cut a video and upload it to share it with the fidget spinner community.

What a fidget spinner can't do for you

- **Help with ADHD:** You see a lot of ads hyping fidget spinners as the best cure for ADHD, autism, anxiety, and stress, but science doesn't really back up the use of spinners to help with most of these. So, until you can come in to school with a prescription from a doctor, you can't use a diagnosis as an excuse to bring one into class.

- **Save you $$:** Your spinner obsession can lead you down an expensive road. Sure, some spinners cost $1 to $2, but the price tag can get pretty high—into the tens of thousands, believe it or not!

- **Earn points with your teacher:** Many schools are banning spinners because they're distracting and can be dangerous. If fidget spinners are on the do-not-bring list, leave yours at home.

Eight reasons people can't get enough

Fidget spinners . . .

1. Are great for stress relief
2. Are a cinch to learn, and it's not all that hard to master most cool tricks
3. Are good conversation starters
4. Are low-tech and help you unplug
5. Are inexpensive, especially if you make your own
6. Keep you from dismembering pens or picking at your hair or fingernails
7. Are fun to play with
8. Are a lot less annoying than bottle flipping (maybe)

Five reasons parents and teachers want to throw fidget spinners out the window

Fidget spinners . . .

1. Are distracting to other people when you use them
2. Can keep you from paying attention when you use them
3. Can be addictive
4. Can be dangerous if thrown or dropped while performing a trick
5. Had a purpose before they became a toy—to help people with special needs

QUIZ: WHAT TYPE OF FIDGETER ARE YOU?

There are many different styles of fidget spinners out there, and there are just as many types of people who spin! But what type of fidget spinner are you? Take this quick quiz to find out.

1. **When I got my first fidget spinner . . .**
   a. Everyone else already had one
   b. I was the first person I knew who had heard of them
   c. I had seen people do tricks and needed to have one
   d. I made it myself

2. **I use my spinner . . .**
   a. When I have nothing better to do
   b. When I should be eating, sleeping, or doing my homework
   c. In front of a mirror so I can practice my moves
   d. In front of my notepad so I can test, record, and refine my creations

3. **When it comes to tricks . . .**
   a. I can do a couple
   b. I know every trick in the book and practice them constantly
   c. People stop to stare and applaud when I'm done
   d. Check out my YouTube channel, along with all my other subscribers

4. **I use a fidget spinner because . . .**
   a. It's something to do with my hands
   b. I want to keep getting better at tricks and break lots of records
   c. I'm completely obsessed with it—it's my life
   d. I'm fascinated with perfecting my spinner collection

Results: If you got . . .

Mostly As: You're a **casual fidgeter**. You like the craze but only until the next cool thing comes along. Fidget spinners are not going to become part of your life story.

Mostly Bs: You're a **devoted fidgeter**. You have embraced the fidget spinner and all of its shining, spinning potential for fun. You have a bright future ahead of you for about a week as a YouTube star.

Mostly Cs: You are **fidget-obsessed**. Fidget spinners are your life, and you'll stick with the craze long after everyone else's spinner is collecting lint at the bottom of their backpack.

Mostly Ds: You are a **mad scientist**. Fidget spinners are cool, but they're just a means to an end for you and your inventive spirit. You plan on becoming a famous inventor or scientist one day.

Rules of the road: A note about safety

As a spinning distraction to fiddle with in the palm of your hand, a fidget spinner doesn't have too much potential for danger. No one's going to make you wear a helmet or knee-pads while you're practicing your tricks. That said, keep these safety tips in mind.

1. Keep spinners away from kids under five years old. Little kids put everything in their mouths. It may seem gross, but it's one of the ways they explore the world. Fidget spinners are considered a "choking hazard" because pieces can come off the toy and get stuck in little kids' throats.

2. Don't trick out your spinner by attaching sharp objects like pencils to it. Most of you will read this and say, "Duh! Of course not." But others—you know who you are—need to be reminded. If that's you, consider yourself warned that this is really dangerous!

3. Practice throwing tricks in a big, open space, clear of any little brothers, pets, fragile objects, windows, open cans of soda, crystal vases . . . you get the picture. What goes up must come down, and these little spinning disks of fun can knock things over, hurt innocent bystanders, and break stuff faster than you can say "reverse leapfrog."

4. When practicing a throwing trick, only toss the spinner as high as your shoulders—any higher and you run a real risk of hitting your eye or chipping a tooth. Your face is fragile and your family thinks you look perfect just the way you are—don't let a fidget spinner rearrange your face.

CHAPTER TWO: ALL ABOUT FIDGET SPINNERS

How it all began

The summer of 1993 was no fun for Catherine Hettinger or her young daughter. Catherine wasn't feeling well and she couldn't play with her daughter, who was getting very fidgety and frustrated. Catherine started making new toys for her daughter out of anything she could get her hands on, like newspaper and tape. As her daughter played with the toys she put together, Catherine made little adjustments here and there and changed the toys to keep making them more interesting.

Patent: a license granted by the government that makes an inventor the only one who can make or sell their invention or prototype.

By spring, Catherine had created a prototype (a basic model) of the spinner, and in 1997 she filed for a patent with the US government. Catherine sold a few spinners and made some money, but in 2005 she decided not to pay the $400 fee to renew the patent. When she released the patent, it allowed anyone who wanted to, to make and sell her design.

Since then, people have used fidget spinners to help curb a need for fidgeting. For example, some people have a physical need to fiddle with something. They sometimes pull out their hair or pick their skin or nails. They click a pen or jiggle their leg. Fidget spinners were seen as a way to let such people quietly fidget in a way that wasn't destructive or loud and didn't bother anyone. Other people use fidget spinners to distract themselves from urges so they could quit smoking or stop other bad habits. And some people use them just to help themselves relax.

Suddenly, in late 2016, fidget spinners started appearing everywhere, and by spring of 2017 it seemed they were in every classroom, store, and public space.

Spinners now come in many shapes, sizes, colors, and materials, and you can make your own very easily using a 3-D printer or random objects you have lying around the house, like LEGO bricks and things you can find in a junk drawer or toolbox.

Kinds of spinners

Standard spinner in gold

Standard spinner: A three-pronged spinner perfectly weighted for long spinning time. The only ball bearing is in the center.

Tri-spinner

Tri-spinner: A three-pronged spinner with ball bearings in each of the spokes as well. Great for tricks and competitions.

Ninja tri-spinner

Ninja tri-spinner: Designed for extended spinning time, the ninja also has ball bearings in each of the spokes. Sharply pronged edges make this design bad for tricks that involve throwing.

Torqbar spinner with a fun, light-up design

Torqbar spinner: The Torqbar is a two-pronged spinner made for long spin time. The balance of the two-pronged design makes it flutter as it spins, creating a more interesting spin and a cooler whooshing sound.

Six sides makes this spinner even more fun

Six-sided spinner: Spinners with six spokes like this only have one bearing in the center. This super cool design makes it whiz fast and even more fun to play with.

Extra-fun spinners

Quad four: A quad four is a spinner with four spokes that has one bearing in the center and one in each spoke.

Wheel: Some designs have zero spokes. They're good for even spinning, fiddling, and throwing tricks that don't involve handling the spinner by its outside edges.

Bat signal: A Torqbar design in the shape of the bat signal, the bat-style spinner usually has bearings in the spokes as well as the center, making it better for tricks and everyday fun. It also looks hella cool.

What to look for in a good spinner

Removable buttons: A screw-off or pop-off locking mechanism so you can remove the buttons (also known as caps) and clean the ball bearings.

Standard bearings: R188 stainless steel ten-ball bearings let you unscrew the buttons and swap them with other spinners for a fresh look.

EDC: Spinners labeled with EDC are for Every-Day-Carry, meaning they fit comfortably in the palm of your hand and in your pocket and they're not too rare or expensive for everyday use.

Balanced weight: If you can hold the spinner in your hand before buying it—since most spinners are purchased online or come in packages, that isn't always possible—check the weight in your hand and make sure it feels balanced. If you can actually try a spin before you buy, even better!

Looks: Don't settle for the first spinner you see. Spinners come in many colors, styles, and finishes. And if you don't see one you like, you can always make your own!

Spinner anatomy lesson

Fidget spinners, made from plastic, wood, metal, or even clay, with a center that rotates and several prongs that spin around it, are intended for mindless play while working or sitting in class. But if that's all there were to the story, you wouldn't be so obsessed with it, would you?

Frame
The frame is the basic shell of the spinner that the bearings fit into. They can be made of plastic, metal, wood, or clay, and can even be custom printed using a 3-D printer.

Center bearing

The center contains a machine called a bearing, which reduces friction to make the fidget spinner rotate more quickly. Each spoke usually contains its own bearing as well, letting the spokes spin just as freely. Different kinds of bearings cause spinners to behave in different ways, adjusting for vibration, noise, and spin time.

Spokes

Most spinners have three spokes, but some have two and others have more. Some spokes have bearings of their own for side-spinning action, while others just act as weights.

Buttons

Most spinners come with buttons, or caps, covering the center bearing. These buttons are almost always removable. Some tricks require the buttons to stay on—like when you're balancing the spinner on a flat surface like a table, book, or random body part. Other tricks are better when you remove the cap, like when you pinch the spinner between two fingers or insert a pencil or another sharp object into the center hole.

Buttons on inexpensive plastic fidget spinners need to be popped off with either a flathead screwdriver or a solid flat lever. The first time you pry them off will be the hardest. After repeated removals, the buttons will be looser and you can pry them off with your fingers.

Pricier spinners have buttons that twist off. To remove them, hold one side with one hand and twist the other until it comes apart.

Tip: If your spinner started out spinning for minutes at a time and now its spin time is reduced, the bearings could be clogged. Pop over to the Troubleshooting section in Chapter Five for cleaning tips to get your spinner running as good as new —or even better!

Tip: If your spinner wobbles or spins for only a few seconds on its first try out of the box, tighten the center buttons. If you've had it a while and it doesn't perform like it used to, try cleaning the ball bearings. Your spinner probably spends a lot of time in your pocket and on the ground, so it's bound to collect a lot of dust, dirt, and gunk.

THE PHYSICS BEHIND THE PHUN

Fidget spinners are cool on their own, but as you play, you're actually learning science! Check out these *phabulous physics phacts* that may help you ace a test or plan your next science fair project.

Sir Isaac Newton, the father of modern physics, explained motion, gravity, and force in terms of three basic laws.

Law 1: An object at rest or in motion will stay at rest or in motion unless acted upon by an outside force.

A spinner sitting motionless on the table will stay motionless until you apply torque or force by flicking the spoke and spinning it.

Isaac Newton

Law 2: How fast an object speeds up or slows down depends on how big the object is and how much force you use to make it move or stop moving.

It takes more energy to spin a big spinner than a small spinner. Spinners with longer spokes spin differently than those with shorter spokes, and spinners with heavier and lighter spokes spin differently as well.

Law 3: For every action, there is an equal and opposite reaction.

The spinner cuts through the air and the air pushes back on it. The spinner will keep going as long as you keep pushing the spoke to keep it spinning. Once you stop putting pressure on the spinner, the air resistance will eventually push back enough that the spinner will stop.

Force is a push or pull on an object that comes from the object's *interaction* with another object—in this case, air, dirt, or your hand, for example.

The force that's used to flick the spinner and start the spinning is called *torque*. Torque is the amount of force acting on an object that causes that object to rotate. You can flick the spinner harder, with more torque, to increase the speed and make it spin longer.

Take away friction and the spinner will spin longer

At the core of every fidget spinner is a bearing, a center ring that lets the spinner go for minutes at a time without stopping. Bearings can be composed of different materials, such as ceramic and metal. Good bearings help the spinner spin longer and faster. Fidget spinners use wheel bearings like the ones you find on skateboard wheels to reduce *friction* and move smoothly.

> (i) *Friction*: the force that makes objects stop moving when they touch each other.

The bearing is made up of two circles: the inner circle is held at rest with your fingers, and the outer circle (the bearing race) rotates around the inner circle while it slides across the small moving balls inside. Since this outer circle slides around the inner circle on rotating balls instead of sliding on the surface of the inner circle, friction is reduced. This lets the spinner keep rotating for a long time.

All good spins must come to an end

What makes it stop? Why doesn't a spinner spin forever?

According to Newton's first law, if the spinner is in motion, it will continue to stay in motion as long as there are no outside forces on it, like your hand stopping it, basic air resistance pushing back on it, or dirt getting in the way of the bearings.

According to the third law, when the bearings meet with friction, they experience torque in the opposite direction than the spinner is rotating. This frictional torque acts to slow down the spinner and eventually make it stop.

All spinners are not created equal

Spinners can be made out of different materials and come in many shapes and sizes. Even though most fidget spinners have ball bearings, they all behave differently. Some spin for longer, some spin more smoothly, and some are better for tricks or random pocket fidgeting.

What makes spinners behave so differently? That can be answered with Newton's second law: How fast an object speeds up or slows down depends on how big the object is and how much force you use to make it move or stop moving.

Spokes can be long or short, heavy or light. The way a spinner is weighted has a huge effect on how it spins.

Think of a bicycle. The faster you pedal, the faster you go. If you're going uphill, you have to work harder to go at the same speed. If the ball bearings get dirty, or if you blow against the direction the spinner is going, it's like going uphill or pedaling against a strong headwind.

PRICE MATCH: Believe it or not, the price of the spinner doesn't always match its performance. One-dollar spinners can spin evenly for minutes at a time and be great for tricks while a $50 spinner may just look cool and not spin very well.

The location of the center button makes it easy to get the spokes spinning. If it were off-center, it would wobble. That's why the design and manufacture of the spinner is so important to how it works.

The physics of sound: Why spinners hum when they spin

A sound wave is produced by varying air pressure. When a spinner spins, it moves the air quickly, causing a small change in air pressure. When these variations in air pressure reach your ear, they make your eardrum vibrate at the same rate the air pressure is varying by, creating sound.

In some spinners, you're also hearing sound generated by the rolling ball bearings.

When you blow on a spinner, not only can you get it to move, depending on the direction and force of your breath, but you can also create some pretty neat sounds!

Experiments to try

Can you see with your ears?

Close your eyes and have a friend spin the spinner and move it around. See if you can point to the spinner. How can you tell where it is?

The *Doppler effect* is well known to anyone who has ever stood at the side of a busy street, waiting for the light to change. You can tell by the sound the cars make whether they are coming toward you or moving away. The sound is louder when it's closest to you and it changes as it moves away. Your ears are very experienced instruments of sound detection. Working with your brain, your ears will be able to tell you fairly easily where the spinning spinner is if you listen carefully.

Can you make a spinner appear to reverse direction?

Hold the spinner sandwiched between two fingers, with your middle finger on top and your thumb on the bottom, and spin it clockwise while you hold it. Next, flip the spinner upside-down. It appears to reverse direction and spin counterclockwise.

How did you get it to magically change direction? The answer is that you didn't. It's an optical illusion. When you turn the spinner upside-down, you're just looking at it from the opposite direction. Imagine you have a transparent clock face with a second hand, and you see it going clockwise. Turn it over and it continues going in the same direction. From your new point of view (or perspective), it's going counter-clockwise, even though the direction of spin doesn't actually change.

Experiment with Newton's laws

When you hold the spinner sandwiched between two fingers, just like in the optical illusion above, and you twist your hand left and right, forward and back, you can feel the weight distribution shift in the spinner in your hand. It feels almost as if the spinner wants to be moved in a circle.

When this happens, it's called *angular momentum*. This goes back to Newton's laws. The spinner wants to keep going in its present direction. If you twist it, you're changing its direction, which takes applying force. It's resisting your efforts.

"PLAY IS THE HIGHEST FORM OF RESEARCH."
—ALBERT EINSTEIN

You know more science than you think

Many tricks involve throwing and catching the spinner while it spins. Have you ever stopped to wonder how your brain can do such complicated calculations to decide exactly where the spinner will fall? The math would be almost impossible to calculate. You have to take into account the size and weight of the spinner, the force with which you're throwing it, the direction you're throwing it in, and the current air pressure, just to name a few variables. But somehow, your brain can figure out automatically how to throw it just right and how to catch it without doing any math!

The reason is muscle memory. Your brain records everything it sees, hears, and experiences. You've seen things go up and come down. You've thrown and caught many things in the past. Your body draws on those experiences and basically makes an educated guess!

That's why practice makes perfect. When you watch people do tricks and practice them on your own, you're teaching your mind and body how to act and react and make better predictions.

With that in mind, let's head to the next chapter and start practicing some of those cool, mind-expanding tricks!

"SCIENCE IS SIMPLY COMMON SENSE AT ITS BEST."
—THOMAS HUXLEY

CHAPTER THREE: TRICKS OF THE TRADE

Master the art of fidget spinning . . . one awesome trick at a time

Show your stuff with these awesome fidget-spinning tricks! Whether you just want some fun tips for easy fidget spinning or you're all about taking your skills to the extreme, these tricks have a little bit of everything. Use the stars as your guide—from one to five—to find the tricks that range from a fidget spinning cakewalk to crazy ones that'll bring you to fidget spinning glory.

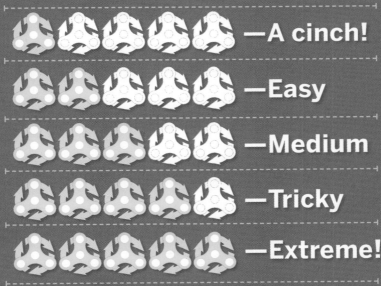

DIFFICULTY SCALE

Take a look at the spinners next to each trick. Start with the easy breezy ones or move all the way up to five spinners show your master-class fidget spinner skills!

—A cinch!

—Easy

—Medium

—Tricky

—Extreme!

Tip: To practice a catching trick, master it without spinning first. Once you have the catch down, give it a spin.

LEVEL 1: START YOUR ENGINES

Any trick starts with a spin, and getting it spinning well is half the fun of a fidget spinner. Here are a few ways to get yours going.

BASIC TABLE SPIN:

This is the easiest way to get started and watch how your spinner works.

1. Place the spinner on a table.
2. Put your pointer finger of one hand on the center to hold it steady.
3. Spin with the pointer of your other hand.

Start your spinner adventure with the Basic Table Spin!

BASIC SPIN:

You can't become a pro until you master the basics!

1. Hold the spinner between your finger and thumb.
2. Spin it with the pointer of your other hand.

Watch the colors of the spinner swirl together with the Basic Spin!

OPEN FACE:

This one is also known as the "finger spin." Each finger gets a little bit harder, so try your best to switch between each one. Some fingers are harder than others.

Finger difficulty from easiest to hardest:

Thumb | Middle finger | Pointer | Ring finger | Pinky

1. Balance the spinner on the pad or fleshy part of one finger and spin it.

Start with your pointer finger.

Then try your middle finger.

Tip: When you're just learning finger tricks, balance the spinner on the pad of your thumb. Once you master that skill, try balancing and spinning it on the pads of your other fingers.

Move on to your ring finger.

Then try your pinky!

PLATE SPINNER:

Perform the Open Face trick on the tip of your finger instead of the pad. Lighter-weight spinners work best for balancing on smaller targets.

Start by trying it on your thumb.

Now your pointer finger: it's like twirling a basketball!

Now move on to the middle finger.

The ring finger gets even trickier —see if you can master it!

If you can spin on the pinky, you're a master.

KNUCKLE SPIN:

Ramp up your skills by trying these spins on the back of your hand, using your knuckles as a guide.

1. Hold your hand out flat, palm facing down.
2. Balance the spinner on one of your knuckles.
3. Give it a gentle spin.

Let it whirl.

FLICK START:

This is an easy yet flashy way to start a trick. You can flick your spinner using just about anything!

1. Hold the spinner between your finger and thumb.
2. Flip the edge against your leg or a piece of furniture to start it spinning.

Flick the spinner off of your leg or another surface to get it spinning!

REVERSE:

The cool part about this trick is that when you flip the spinner, it looks like it changes direction. But the spinner is still going the same way, just upside-down!

1. Spin it between two fingers, with your middle finger on top.
2. Flip your hand over so your thumb is on top.

YOUR BIGGEST FAN:

Look, no hands! Watch how wind speed gets the spinner moving.

1. Balance the spinner on a table or between your fingers.
2. Turn on a hair dryer at its coolest setting and aim it at the spinner to get it moving.

"THE SECRET OF GETTING AHEAD IS GETTING STARTED."
—MARK TWAIN

LEVEL 2: ARE YOU READY FOR SOME COOL TRICKS?

KNUCKLE GRAB:

It's one thing to let the spinner spin on your hand, it's another to watch it flip in the air.

1. Perform the knuckle spin.
2. Flick your hand up to toss the spinner lightly into the air.
3. Catch it as it comes back down.

Start by balancing the spinner on your knuckles, palm facedown.

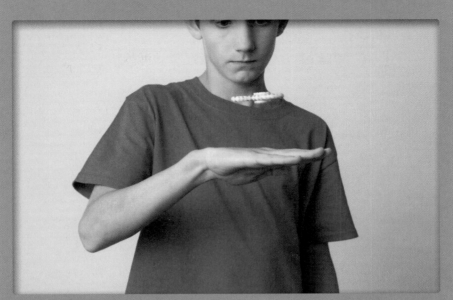

Toss it up!

Let it land back down. **Pro tip:** It's easier to catch if you lower your hand gently along with the spinner as it drops back down. Keeping your hand rigidly in the same spot will make it bounce off.

Tip: Amp up the knuckle grab by catching the spinner while it's still spinning!

KNUCKLE SANDWICH:

You've have a chance to try out some knuckle tricks. Got them down? Good! Now try it again, but this time catch it on your knuckle and keep it spinning!

1. Perform the knuckle grab.
2. Catch it between two fingers.
3. Flip it back up and catch it on the back of your hand.

Start by balancing the spinner on your knuckles, palm facedown.

Snatch it in midair!

Tip: Keep the center in place for any tricks where you're tossing and catching the spinner to make the skill easier to master.

CONVERTIBLE:

Let the top down with this trick, which is all about balance.

1. Spin it between your thumb and middle finger.
2. Take the top finger off, letting it spin out in the fresh air.

Hold the spinner horizontally with your thumb and middle finger.

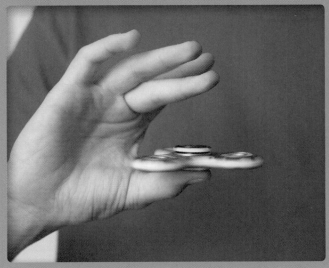

Raise your finger up to let it ride free!

THE ZIPPER:

The faster you shake your arm, the faster it will spin in this cool trick. Use a smaller spinner for the very best performance.

1. Hold the spinner by an outer frame weight between your thumb and middle finger.
2. Shake your hand at the elbow to flip the spinner up.
3. Try to get the spinner to spin, passing through the hole between your fingers and your palm.

Spin it as fast as you can through this space in your hand.

Tip: Can't fit the spinner between your fingers and your palm? Try your other hand. Your non-dominant hand has less muscle mass and you may have a little more room to work with.

HAND TWIST:

The Hand Twist may as well be performance art. The cool arm motion makes you look like you're working some spinner magic.

1. Spin the spinner between your middle finger and thumb.
2. Hold it up like you're holding a sandwich at a fancy tea party.
3. Twist your wrist so your hand passes under your elbow, close to your body.
4. Then wrap it back around while it's still spinning.

Start with the spinner in midair in front of you.

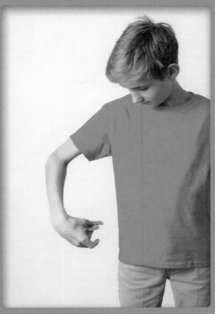

Keeping the spinner between the thumb and middle finger, bring it underneath your elbow.

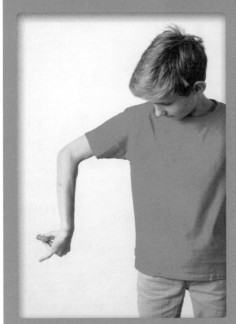

Twist it around.

Then bring it back to the front!

HOT POTATO:

This trick will test your reflexes. Focus on your control as you toss it back and forth between your hands while it spins.

1. Toss the spinner from hand to hand while it's spinning.

Tip: Bending your knees when you toss the spinner makes it a little easier.

Start with the spinner in one hand.

Toss it like it's hot!

Catch it on the other side.

THE CATCH:

Once you've mastered the catch, try tossing it even higher to keep the challenge going.

1. Perform a basic spin between your thumb and middle finger.
2. Turn it sideways so your spinner is vertical (taller than it is wide).
3. Toss it into the air and catch it.

Start it sideways for a trickier flip.

Toss it as high as you can!

Catch it sideways in the opposite hand.

TABLE DARTS:

For this dart game, use a spinner that has bearings on its spokes. This will let you do all sorts of fun catches, perfecting your hand-eye coordination as you use your pencil as a dart.

1. Perform the basic table spin.
2. Hold a pencil above it and jab the pencil at the spinner.
3. Catch the pencil in a spoke hole to make it stop spinning.

FACE SPINS:

This one doesn't need much explanation. Just be careful when you use your face as the playing field for your spinner!

1. Tilt your head back and balance the spinner on your nose, forehead, or chin.
2. Give it a spin!

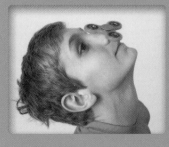

Tilt your head back so the spinner can balance on the tip of your nose.

Balance it on your forehead—it's a no brainer.

Keep your chin up! Carefully tilt your head back to get just the right balance.

CALL A TOE TRUCK:

Test your balance (and your flexibility!) as you use your toes as a landing dock for your spinner.

1. Sit with your legs out in front of you.
2. Balance a spinner on your big toe and give it a whirl.

Tip: Try your elbow next!

THE CEILING FAN:

For this trick, you'll need a long dowel. A broom or mop with a flat handle top works well, too. Once you get it moving, voilà! A ceiling fan!

1. Spin the spinner, then carefully transfer it to the top of the dowel.
2. Slowly raise the dowel up until the spinner touches the ceiling while it's still spinning.

Balance the spinner carefully on the top of the dowel.

Keep it spinning until it's as high as the ceiling!

THE GYROSCOPE:

Amaze your friends and family as your fidget spinner defies gravity. For this trick, you'll need to get your spinner rotating fast. You'll also need a pencil with an eraser, a piece of paper on a flat surface, and masking tape, as well as a tri-spinner with a center that has removable buttons. The spinner has to fit close to the center without moving up or down, so you'll need to bulk up the pencil to keep it in place.

1. Pop out the center button.
2. Wind masking tape around the pencil about two inches from the bottom.
3. Slide the spinner onto the pencil so it's sitting on the masking tape, then wind another piece of tape above the spinner.
4. Make sure the spinner can spin freely but doesn't move up or down along the pencil.
5. Place a piece of paper on a flat table.
6. Hold the pencil, eraser side down, on the paper and spin the spinner.
7. As long as the spinner is rotating quickly, the pencil will stay up.

Tape up the pencil about two inches from the bottom.

Place the spinner over the tape.

No hands! The Gyro gets amazing spinning action all on its own.

Tip: Mastered the Gyroscope trick? Now try spinning it on a water bottle cap or the tip of your finger.

LEVEL 3: IN IT TO WIN IT

Toss, catch, and perform open spins to take your fidget skills to the next level. The best way to master these three-star tricks is to practice, practice, practice!

> "WE ARE WHAT WE REPEATEDLY DO. EXCELLENCE, THEREFORE, IS NOT AN ACT BUT A HABIT."
> —ARISTOTLE

ONE POTATO, TWO POTATO:

A little trickier than the hot potato, this one has you tossing the spinners in opposite directions. It will take a few tries to nail this one, but once you do, you're on your way to being a spinner extraordinaire.

1. Hold one spinner in each hand and toss the spinners into the air at the same time.
2. Catching them with the opposite hand as if you're juggling them.

Hold the spinners up.

Get them spinning.

Toss them in the air!

Catch them with opposite hands!

DOUBLE CATCH:

Amp up your game! How high can you toss these spinners and still catch them both?

1. Using two spinners, perform the Basic Spin with a spinner in each hand.
2. Turn them both sideways, and toss both into the air.
3. Catch both at the same time.

FINGER TWIST:

This is just like the hand twist, but instead of spinning the spinner between two fingers, you're performing it with an open face. It's almost like you're holding a tray or spinning a basketball. The trick is to keep the spinner level so it doesn't tilt or fall.

1. Perform the Hand Twist with an Open Face.
2. Pass your hand around, close to your body and under your elbow.

Spin it on your fingertip.

Bring it down low.

Spin it around the back.

Bring it back to the front!

FINGER HOP:

Hop that spinner around from one finger to another!

1. Spin the spinner on your pointer.
2. Toss it up in the air.
3. Catch it with the next finger on the same hand.

Start your hop with the pointer finger.

Now move it along to your middle finger.

Raise the stakes with the ring finger.

Hop all the way to the pinky, if you can!

LEAP FROG:

Leap across from one finger to the other, but don't croak!

1. Toss the spinner from your pointer finger on one hand to the pointer on your other hand.

FACE PASS:

Rather than placing the spinner on your face and then spinning, this trick has the spinner already in motion as you pass it along. Just be careful to keep balance so the spinner doesn't hit you.

1. Spin the spinner on your fingertip.
2. Transfer it, still spinning, to your nose or chin.

LEVEL 4: PRO SPINS

Keep those spinners spinning as you switch positions, fingers, and hands in these show-off-worthy tricks.

> "HAVE PATIENCE WITH ALL THINGS, BUT FIRST OF ALL WITH YOURSELF."
> —SAINT FRANCIS DE SALES

LEAP FROG RELAY:

Just like the Leap Frog, but with more endurance. Leap back and forth between the pointer fingers. Challenge yourself by picking up speed or tracking how many hops you can do successfully.

1. Toss it back and forth between your two pointer fingers.
2. See how many times you can go back and forth.

ZIP AND FLIP:

This spin requires you to get a good, fast spin going. See how high you can toss it before you catch it again!

1. Hold the spinner by an outer frame weight and perform the zipper, spinning it between your middle finger and thumb.
2. Get it spinning fast.
3. Toss the spinner up and catch it by the center between your thumb and middle finger.

Get a good spinning rhythm before you toss it up!

BEHIND-THE-BACK TOSS:

This looks cool with a basketball, but even cooler with a spinner. Practice this one for big wow factor.

1. Spin the spinner between two fingers and pass it behind your back.
2. Toss it gently into the air and reach around your back.
3. Catch it again in the same hand or the opposite hand.

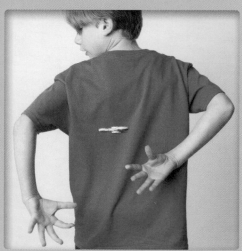

Let your spinner take flight!

ONE-WAY STREET:

Head down this street to become a spinner master. It's tricky at first, but when you get it under control, you'll be super savvy with your spinner skills.

1. Hop the spinner from your pointer to your middle finger, then ring finger and pinky.
2. Flip it up.
3. Catch it between your thumb and middle finger.

DOUBLE SWITCH:

A little bit like juggling, the double switch is a crowd-pleaser. You should end up with your wrists crossed in front of you, with your left hand holding the spinner on your right and your right hand holding the spinner on your left.

1. Perform the Double Catch, but cross your wrists after you throw the spinners in the air.
2. Catch the spinners with the opposite hands.

Toss 'em up!

Catch 'em on the other side!

LEVEL 5: TAKE IT TO THE EXTREME!

ROUND TRIP:

Head toward your final destination of greatness with the Round Trip. As you master each hop, you'll be sure to land on spinner glory.

1. Hop the spinner from finger to finger, starting with your pointer and ending at your pinky.
2. Hop it back until you reach your pointer.
3. Toss it and catch it between your thumb and middle finger.

PUDDLE JUMPER:

The Leap Frog Relay had you hopping from one lily pad to the other, but this one makes the gap even bigger and you'll be traveling between islands of spinner fun.

1. Perform the Leap Frog Relay by tossing the spinner back and forth between your fingers.
2. Widen the distance between your hands each time you make a catch.

Get it spinning on one hand.

With a wide stance, toss it to the other side.

Catch it with the other, and challenge yourself with a wider stance each time!

TELEPORT:

Consider yourself a master if you can do this trick! Start slow and focus on balance before working your way up to speedy spinning.

1. Perform the Round Trip.
2. Then toss it, still spinning, from your pointer to the pointer of your other hand.
3. Continue going up and back again.

MULTIPLE-SPINNER TRICKS

GOT MORE THAN ONE? HOW MANY CAN YOU USE AT ONE TIME?

"IF YOU CAN DREAM IT,
YOU CAN DO IT."
—WALT DISNEY

THE DOUBLE:

Get ambidextrous and try out a spinner in each hand!

1. Spin one in each hand between your thumb and middle finger.

THE STACKER:

How many can you spin at once? This trick looks cool but is super easy to master!

1. Pop out the center and line up multiple spinners on a pencil or pen.
2. Hold it up and give it a spin.

See how many you can stack!

THE REVERSE STACKER:

Just like The Stacker, but with a little switcheroo.

1. Keep the center buttons in on two spinners.
2. Stack them on top of each other, button-to-button, and hold them between your thumb and middle finger.
3. Spin the top spinner clockwise and spin the bottom spinner counterclockwise (in the other direction).

Stack and spin!

THE TABLETOP:

Watch one spinner on top of the other and see how cool it looks!

1. Stack one spinner on top of another.
2. Spin the top spinner.

BUNK BEDS:

The two spinners going in opposite directions will make for really cool optics. Just don't get dizzy!

1. Stack one spinner on top of another.
2. Spin the top spinner in one direction and the bottom spinner in the opposite direction.

THE DOUBLE DOUBLE:

This gets a little trickier. Test your balance and your coordination as you get these spinners going.

1. Spin a stack of two spinners on each pointer finger.

Get the spinners moving one on top of the other.

Lift your thumbs up and watch them go!

THE OLD SWITCHEROO:

See what happens when you touch moving spinners together!

1. Perform the double.
2. Touch the spinners to each other and make them change direction.

By touching each other while in motion, the spinners force each other in opposite directions.

PASS THE TORCH:

No need to touch or flick the spinner on your own—the movement from the first spinner will get the other one in motion!

1. Spin the first in one hand and bring the second one close to it, between your thumb and middle finger.
2. Let the first one "light" the second by touching it.

Touch one moving spinner to a still spinner to get it going.

DOUBLE FACE SPIN:

Get fancy with two spinners on your face at the same time. Just be careful to balance the spinners so that they don't hit you.

1. Balance one spinning spinner on your nose.
2. Balance one on your chin at the same time.

THE SANDWICH:

This is a massive spinner sandwich that looks super cool, but probably doesn't taste very good. How many spinners can you spin on one hand at one time?

1. Stack three or more spinners between your thumb and finger.
2. Spin the top spinner clockwise, the middle one counterclockwise, and the bottom one clockwise.

This is a whopper of a spin!

CHAPTER FOUR: GAME TIME

Competitive spinning

Fidget spinners are fun to play with solo, but there's no limit to what you can do to make spinning even more fun. Play these games with friends to make the most of your fidget spinner skills, or even come up with your own! Keep score by tracking your time, points, and the level of difficulty as you go.

> **"I FEAR NOT THE MAN WHO HAS PRACTICED 10,000 KICKS ONCE. BUT I FEAR THE MAN WHO HAS PRACTICED ONE KICK 10,000 TIMES."**
> **—BRUCE LEE**

Fidget spinner field goal

Face off against an opponent to see who can shoot five field goals with their spinner first.

You'll need:

- ✓ Two players
- ✓ One spinner
- ✓ A table
- ✓ Masking tape
- ✓ A 2x1 LEGO brick or a jelly bean to serve as the football

Set up the playing field: Mark out two goals of equal size on the table surface in front of you using the masking tape.

To play

Face each other at opposite ends of the table. Decide who will shoot first by seeing who can spin the spinner the longest.

To shoot, place the spinner in front of your own goal at one end of the table, with your finger on top of the button. Spin the spinner and don't move it from that spot.

Once the spokes of the spinner are moving, give the football a light push into the spokes of the spinner. The force of the spinning spokes will push the football across the table—hopefully in the direction of your opponent's goal!

Tip: Make sure the football stays in contact with the table at all times. Don't move the spinner from your goal when you're shooting.

If your football makes it through the field goal, you get a point. Take turns shooting the ball at each other's goal. The first person to score five points wins.

Fidget spinner hockey

In this game, your spinning spinner is your hockey stick.

"CHAMPIONS KEEP PLAYING UNTIL THEY GET IT RIGHT."
—BILLIE JEAN KING

You'll need:

- ✓ Two players
- ✓ Two spinners with only one button removed
- ✓ Two pencils
- ✓ A table
- ✓ Masking tape
- ✓ A 2x1 LEGO brick or jelly bean to serve as the hockey puck

Set up the playing field: Mark out two goals of equal size on the table surface in front of you using the masking tape.

Pop out the top button on each spinner and insert a pencil into the top hole of each. This becomes your hockey stick. Control the spinner by moving your hockey stick around the table.

To play

Flip a coin to see who gets to bring the puck into play. To begin, get your spinners moving and bring them out onto the playing field. The first player hits the puck from their home goal area into the center "ice" to bring it into play. Once the puck is in play, hit it with your stick to shoot it toward your opponent's goal. Your opponent will also be wielding a spinning hockey stick and will try to block your shots and hit the puck into your goal at the same time.

If your spinner stops rotating, quickly get it spinning again—there are no time-outs for stationary spinners! The first player to score five points wins.

Minute to win it challenges

Set a timer and challenge yourself or a friend to see what you can accomplish in a minute.

- How many spinning catches can you complete?
- How many spinners can you spin on a tabletop at once?
- Can you complete a behind-the-back toss and a spinning catch in less than a minute?
- Can you get two spinners spinning on a table at one time using only one hand?

Head-to-head competition

How does your best spinner perform against your friend's? Try these head-to-head challenges. Keep track of wins, losses, and records in the charts at the back of this book.

Here are a few things you can compare:

- Which spinner spins on the tabletop for longer?
- Who can spin on one finger for longer?
- Who can perform the most catches as you toss it from hand to hand?
- Whose spinner can balance on the corner of a cell phone or book for longer?
- Spin your spinners side by side on a wooden floor. With your thumb on top of the spinner, flick it across the floor. Whose traveled the farthest?
- Spin a spinner. Stack wooden Jenga tiles on top of it as it spins. Who can stack the most tiles on top without making it all come tumbling down?
- Who can spin the most spinners on their fingers at once?
- Who can build the best spinner out of LEGOs?

"PLAY IS OUR BRAIN'S FAVORITE WAY OF LEARNING."—DIANE ACKERMAN

Group and party games

Even though spinners were designed for solo use, they're even more fun with friends! Practicing your solo spinner tricks is a lot of fun, but how about tricks you can do together?

Can you:

- Spin a spinner and toss it to your friend in a spinning catch?
- Spin it on the back of your hand, flick your hand, and have your friend catch it?
- See how many times you can toss it between you while it's still spinning, stepping back each time to widen the distance?
- Fist-bump a friend and pass a spinning spinner? To do this, close your hand into a loose fist and spin the spinner on the back of your hand at your knuckle. Gently bump fists with your friend and pass the spinner, still spinning. Best way to greet a friend ever!

Party games

Fidget spinners put a new spin on party games! Hand out fidget spinners as a favor at the beginning of the party, decorate them to personalize everyone's spinner, and spend your time playing party games like these.

Line up: Line up side by side and toss a spinning fidget spinner back and forth, just like in a water balloon toss, stepping back one step after each successfully completed toss.

Hot potato: Stand in a circle. Start the spinner. Quickly pass it around the circle, keeping it spinning. When the spinner stops or drops, the last person to touch it is out. Keep it going until there's only one person left.

Mannequin challenge: Remove the center, then balance spinners on top of posts or your friends' fingers and try to spin as many as you can at once. Have everyone stand still and pose as long as the spinners keep spinning. Make sure you have someone on hand to capture this trick on video.

Relay race: Create two teams with half of the people at the starting line and the other half across the room. The starter calls out "Take your marks!" and the first person in each line gets ready. "Get set" tells them to place the spinner on their finger or, to make it easier the first go-round, between their thumb and middle finger. When the starter calls out "Spin!", the first person in each line spins the spinner and walks or runs as fast as possible to their teammate at the other side of the room. When the first person reaches the person waiting, they hand off the spinner—still spinning—to them and they're off, back to the start. Continue spinning and relaying back and forth until everyone has had a chance to cross. If the spinner drops or stops spinning, the person has to go back to their starting point and start over. It's okay to spin the spinner as you go to keep it from stopping.

Obstacle course: Lay out an obstacle course where racers need to duck under, step over, or go around obstacles like cones, tires, or flags. Time each racer as they make their way through the course while still holding their spinner out between two fingers, on the back of their hand, or, if you're really advanced, on one finger. The person who finishes the course without dropping or stopping their spinner wins.

> **Tip:** While you're playing, it's okay to either constantly spin the spinner or give it a whirl every now and then to keep it spinning.

CHAPTER FIVE: SPINNER DIY, HACKS, AND ENHANCEMENTS

DIY: MAKING YOUR OWN SPINNERS

Sure, you can buy a spinner at your corner store or online, but making your own is even cooler!

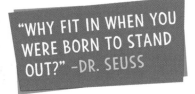

"WHY FIT IN WHEN YOU WERE BORN TO STAND OUT?" –DR. SEUSS

Put a spin on everyday objects with just some glue and parts you probably already have to DIY—Do It Yourself—without using power tools, saws, or other heavy-duty tools that require a lot of safety precautions.

Things you can use:

- ✓ An old skateboard
- ✓ LEGOs
- ✓ Stuff you find in a toolbox
- ✓ Candy
- ✓ A Rice Krispies Treat

Keep these things to keep in mind when making your own spinners:

- **Spinnability:** There needs to be a center that spins smoothly.

- **Balance:** Any item you put on one side has to be perfectly balanced on the other side.

- **Weight:** Your spinner needs to be light enough that you can spin it while holding it, or at least have a base so it can spin on a flat surface like a table or a bottle top.

- **Safety:** Your spinner shouldn't have sharp edges that can cut you as you spin it. The blades are hard to see when they're spinning quickly, and it's just as likely you'll catch a sharp edge as a spot between the spokes if you put your finger in at mid-spin.

SKATEBOARD SPINNER: EASIEST DIY

At its most basic, a fidget spinner is made up of an outer circle that's stationary (doesn't move), an inner circle that does move, and a bearing in the middle. The bearing is made up of about seven or eight metal balls, or about nine ceramic balls, that move to reduce friction between the outer and inner rings. Skateboard wheels spin so smoothly because they work

using this type of bearing. If you have an old skateboard that it's okay to take apart, you can pop out the bearings and spin them between your fingers for a simple fidget.

> **Tip:** If you're reusing an old bearing, you'll need to clean it first. Used bearings are usually greased and are often dirty as well. See the Troubleshooting section for cleaning tips and de-gunk your bearings before proceeding.

Most people don't have a skateboard they want to kill, but fortunately you can buy skateboard bearings from a skateboard store, a big store like Target or Walmart, online at Amazon, or at a sporting goods store.

> **Tip:** There are so many local places to buy skateboard bearings that you don't have to resort to shopping online at stores you've never heard of or pay a lot for shipping. Good skateboard bearings don't need to cost more than $2 each, especially if you buy them in a multipack.

Now add the spokes

Fidgeting with a single bearing is fun, but you can't really do tricks with it until it has spokes.

What you'll need:

- ✓ A ball bearing for the center
- ✓ A hot glue gun
- ✓ Two to four identical items that can act as spokes, such as ball bearings, short KNEX rods, golf tees, or pencil erasers

What to do:

1. Measure the circumference of your ball bearing and place three evenly spaced pencil marks on the outside edge.
2. Place a dab of glue at the first pencil mark and attach the first spoke. Hold it firmly for half a minute until it sets.
3. Attach the other spokes in the same way.
4. Make sure it's completely dry, then start spinning!

> Follow the safety instructions that come with your hot glue gun. Always use a hot glue gun with adult supervision.

BEHOLD, A LEGO SPINNER: THE POSSIBILITIES ARE ENDLESS

If you're at all into LEGOs, you have a few sets and loose pieces lying around. Break out your LEGO box and start poking around. This isn't your ordinary, step-by-step, find-the-perfect-piece-and-snap-them-together kind of instruction. This is an exercise for you to make the ultimate spinner right out of your very own creative and amazing brain. Can you do it? Yes, you can!

> **Tip:** If you have a Ninjago spinner kit, you're already off to a great start! Build your basic spinner, then add spokes at even intervals to get the weight just right. Experiment with long and short, and thin and wide spokes—just make sure every spoke is the same.

> **Tip:** LEGO Technic sets and Mindstorm Gear sets are designed for building simple machines with moving parts. LEGO car sets also have moving parts. These sets usually have axles, plates, wheels, and beams ideal for building the core of your spinner.

Here's what you're looking for:

- ✓ Round plates with a center hole and bumps on top to attach to other LEGOs
- ✓ Gear: a round piece with bumps or "teeth" surrounding a center hole
- ✓ Axle: a long, thin piece that fits into the hole
- ✓ Beam: a long, thin piece with holes (Your beam needs an odd number of holes so the center axle can balance properly; A beam makes a two-spoke spinner)
- ✓ Bricks to create the spokes

Once you've gathered your wheels, experiment with different designs: insert a plate or gear on a center axle and spin it. Attach spokes at even intervals to spin it on its axle. Experiment with more or fewer spokes. Make them long or short. How does it change the balance, speed, and length of time it spins?

If you have a beam, place one axle in the center hole and cap the axle with a round plate. The plate acts as a button, so you can hold it as it spins without friction. Insert an axle or two at each end of your beam and experiment with adding different LEGO bricks to weight the spokes and help it spin.

Tip: Too many possibilities making your head spin? Search online for "LEGO spinners" to see what others have created.

"MIX A LITTLE FOOLISHNESS WITH YOUR SERIOUS PLANS. IT IS LOVELY TO BE SILLY AT THE RIGHT MOMENT."—HORACE

EASY-BREEZY LEGO SPINNER

Sometimes you just don't have the right LEGOs to make your spinner—a wheel might be missing, an axle, or some other part that would be helpful. Don't worry—there's a shortcut! As long as you have wheels and an axle for the center, you can use hot glue to build a super easy LEGO spinner that looks just as cool.

Line up your bricks, including a center wheel.

Glue the bricks to the sides of the center wheel.

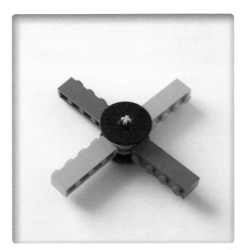

Slide an axle through the center wheel, and cap each side off with the cap that looks like a plastic washer.

TOOLBOX HACK SPINNERS: GOT A BUCKET OF BOLTS? PUT 'EM TO GOOD USE AND GIVE IT A SPIN!

Starting with a center bearing that you've popped out of a skateboard, found lying around the house, or bought for $2 or less, rifle through the bolts, washers, and other odds and ends in your family's toolbox.

Things to look for:

- ✓ Washer: a small, flat disc with a hole in the center
- ✓ Hex nut: a small metal object with a round, threaded center that can screw onto the end of a screw to hold it in place (A hex nut has six flat edges on the outside that are easy to attach to the center bearing or to each other)

A basic toolbox spinner has two, three, or four hex nuts attached around the outside of it. You can use a hot glue gun or Super Glue to attach the nuts to the spinner. Adult supervision is always recommended when using heavy-duty glue.

You only need a few things easy-to-find parts to make your own spinner!

Gluing them together is super easy.

The payoff is a sweet metal spinner that looks heavy-duty. The weight from the spinner will make it go super fast.

Add Some Accents

Take your Toolbox spinner and add some washers to give it an even cooler look.

Find some shiny washers to add to your bolts.

Carefully glue the washers to the bolts.

Come out with a cool-looking spinner!

Tip: Decorate the washers with glow-in-the-dark paint or cool nail polish to jazz up the outside of the spinner.

Make a spinner spin-off

What to do:

(i) "Spin-off:" An imitation of something that's already cool, changed a little to make it even better

1. Make the spokes longer by attaching a second hex nut to the outside of the three main spokes.
2. Attach additional bearings to the end of each hex nut to allow it to spin on more than one axis, making it great for flipping and catching tricks.
3. Glue a washer to the top and bottom of your hex nuts to make them heavier and easier to catch.

QUARTER BLING SPINNER

This is a DIY spinner made out of quarters! For a tri-spinner, you need to make three spokes, each made of two or three quarters. (Three quarters are heavier than two, *obviously*, which makes it easier to spin.) This spinner is a super easy way to make a shiny and fun spinner that'll look extra cool as it spins. If you prefer not to use quarters, you can use metal discs from the hardware store. Ask permission to use a hot glue gun before you start.

This flashy spinner isn't a dime a dozen.

What you'll need:

- ✓ Six or nine quarters
- ✓ Hot glue gun and glue
- ✓ Ball bearing

What to do:

1. Glue the three quarters together in a stack. Do this by placing a dot of hot glue onto both sides of one quarter and sandwiching it evenly between the other two quarters. Do one side at a time so you don't burn yourself.
2. Repeat step 1 for the other two stacks of quarters so you have three separate stacks.

Gather up your loot before starting!

69

3. Place a dot of hot glue on the edge of one of the stacks of quarters. Press the stack against the edge of the ball bearing (horizontally) so that the quarters fan out.

4. Repeat this with the other two stacks of quarters, evenly spacing them around the bearing just like a typical three-sided spinner.

Stack 'em before you spin 'em.

5. Spin!

EDIBLE SPINNERS

You can have your fun and eat it too!

What you'll need:

✓ A silicone putty molding kit (You can buy this online, at a craft store, or in the craft section of a superstore)

> **Tip: Make sure the molding kit you get says "nontoxic" and "food safe"!**

✓ Your favorite spinner
✓ Starburst candies, chocolate, or juice
✓ A plastic knife

What to do:

1. Take off the caps and pop out the bearings of your spinner. Wash and dry your spinner.

2. Prepare the molding putty according to the package directions. Read the directions before you begin to make sure you have everything you need to follow the instructions word for word before the mold starts to harden.

3. Press the spinner base into the mold, set a timer, and wait for it to harden.

4. When it's ready, carefully pop out the spinner. Your mold should have an indentation the exact size and shape of the spinner.

5. Prepare your shell:

- **Starburst:** Unwrap the candy and place it in a bowl. Warm it in the microwave for ten seconds. Remove it from the microwave. If it's the same consistency as dough, it's ready to pop into the mold. If not, put it back into the microwave for ten more seconds. When it's ready, press the candy into the mold and try to keep the top as even as possible.
- **Chocolate:** Place the chocolate in a microwave-safe bowl. Heat it on high power for thirty seconds. Stir. If the chocolate is a smooth liquid, it's ready. If not, keep heating it in the microwave for fifteen seconds at a time and stirring until it's ready, being careful not to overcook it. When it's ready, pour the chocolate into the mold.
- **Juice:** No prep required. Simply pour the juice into the mold.

6. Pop the filled molds into the freezer for at least one hour.
7. Remove the molds from the freezer and touch them to see if they've hardened. When they're ready, carefully remove the filling from the mold.
8. Use a plastic knife to smooth out any rough edges and pop out the center circle so the bearing can fit inside. It's better to cut too little than too much out of the center hole.
9. Pop in the bearing and give it a whirl!

RICE KRISPIES TREAT SPINNER

This one's even easier—no mold required!

What you'll need:

- ✓ A spinner
- ✓ A Rice Krispies Treat
- ✓ A rolling pin
- ✓ A dull knife

What to do:

1. Wash and dry the spinner.
2. Pop out the ball bearing.

The tastiest spinner out there. Just don't eat the center bearing!

You don't need much to make an awesome spinner.

3. Roll the treat with the rolling pin until it's the same thickness as the ball bearing.

4. Place the spinner on top of the treat and press lightly. Using the plastic knife, cut around the outside of the spinner. You now have a spinner-shaped treat!

5. Cut around the center hole, making it just a little smaller than the original hole so it will fit tightly.

6. Pop the ball bearing into the center of the treat so it fits tightly. Press the treat so it molds around the bearing.

7. Stick it in the fridge or let it harden a bit so that the spinner treat gets firm.

8. Give it a spin!

MODS AND HACKS

There are endless possibilities to making your spinner faster, stronger, and cooler. With different mods and hacks, you can take your spinner game to the next level by improving performance or just making it look way more fun. Try out these different techniques to trick out your spinners all on your own.

Troubleshooting your spinner

Before you start tinkering with the spinners you already have, you have to make sure it's working properly. Is your fidget spinner slowing down, wobbling, or not performing like it used to? Since it's a simple machine, the fix is simple, too.

How to be a spin doctor

Adjust the buttons

The caps may be too loose or too tight around your bearing, keeping it from spinning freely. Take them off, wipe the buttons and the bearing with a dry cloth, then put them back on and give it a whirl.

Clean the bearings

Your fidget spinner spends a lot of time in your pocket, on the floor, and in your hands—it's bound to get a little dirty. When dirt gets into the bearings, it creates more friction and stops it from spinning freely. Here's how to clean the bearings:

1. Remove the bearing from the spinner and place it on a paper towel.
2. Spray WD-40 on the ball bearings in the center. WD-40 is a spray-on oil that removes rust and dirt from moving parts and adds water protection, too.
3. Rub the bearing with a paper towel to get the dirt out. Keep rubbing until the towel wipes clean. If your bearings are repurposed from an old skateboard or come from a well-loved spinner, this step may take a while.

4. Fill a small disposable cup with rubbing alcohol. Drop the bearing into the alcohol. Keep it there for half an hour or more.
5. Rinse off the bearing and dry it with a paper towel. Do not use a regular hand towel–fluff and fuzz will get into the bearings and keep it from moving smoothly.
6. Pop the bearing back into your spinner and give it a try!

PERFORMANCE

Bearing swap

Swap out your standard metal bearings for hybrid ceramic bearings for faster, longer spins. You can buy ceramic bearings in packs online. Ceramic bearings have a lower friction coefficient so they spin longer. Many inexpensive spinners can be cheaply upgraded just by swapping in a high-quality bearing.

Tip: Most standard fidget spinners use a 608 miniature bearing.

Button swap

Inexpensive spinners have a button you can pry or pop off. They aren't very efficient: they can make it spin less smoothly, and they can pop off if you drop them while trying tricks. Spinner caps are made with several materials, like brass, aluminum, or steel. They also come in different colors to personalize each of your spinners. Some caps are flat, while others are concave, giving you a dent for resting your fingers. You can find them online, but if you're buying without seeing it first, check the reviews to make sure you're getting exactly what you're paying for.

Tip: Buttons are also called finger caps.

Make catches easier

The caps are a good size for fiddling around with, but if you're practicing difficult throws and catches, a bigger catching surface works like training wheels when you're just getting started. Most caps are around the size of a penny. Stick a quarter on to the each of the caps using glue dots or sticky tack, and your surface is much larger. The quarter face is also ridged, which makes it a little grippier and easier to catch.

Weighted spokes

Weigh down the spokes to help the spinner spin faster and make it easier to control. One way to do this is to add a second set of ball bearings to each spoke. To trick out a tri-spinner, for example, you'll need to either remove the outside bearings from a second spinner or buy three extra bearings.

What you'll need:

- ✓ One tri-spinner
- ✓ Three extra ball bearings

What to do:

1. Push out the bearings on the outer spokes so they're sticking out halfway.
2. Pop a second bearing into the hole of each spoke so each hole now has two bearings sandwiched together.
3. Give it a spin and see the difference the extra weight makes!

Make it silent

Taking off the buttons should reduce most of the noise. You can also try cleaning the bearings, as even the smallest specks of dust or dirt can add a rattle or whirr to a usually quiet spinner.

Make it lighter

Take the bearings out of the spokes on your tri-spinner to make it lighter. It won't spin as long or as fast, but it may help you perfect some of the catching tricks.

Quarter bling weighted spoke

Use quarters to add weight and major coolness to your spinner! Adding weight to the outside spokes also makes the spinner easier to spin. With permission from your parents, use a hot glue gun to glue a quarter to each of the spokes on your spinner. The quarters should come about halfway off the edges of the spokes, as if they were an extension of them. In addition to adding weight for optimal spinning, it'll also make the spinner easier to catch when you do tricks. If you prefer not to glue money to the spinner (because it won't come off again without possibly breaking the spinner), you can use flat metal discs from the hardware store for the same cool effect!

PAINTING YOUR SPINNER

When you paint your spinner, always remove the cap and bearings unless otherwise instructed. Always start with a clean, dry spinner.

Here are some safety rules to follow anytime you use paint:

- Paint your spinners outdoors so you are safe from paint fumes
- Cover your area with a disposable drop cloth, newspapers, or cardboard
- When spray painting, always wear a mask to keep from breathing in the fumes
- Wear disposable gloves to keep the paint from getting on your fingers
- Hold spray paint cans at least one foot from the spinner
- Always be sure to point the spray away from your face and body

Cool splatter effects makes your spinner totally unique!

Use a plastic knife or an old toothbrush to make cleanup easy.

SPLATTER PAINT

Make a splash with some flash! Splatter one color or a few to trick out and personalize your one-of-a-kind masterpiece. Choose your favorite colors, or the colors of your favorite sports teams!

What you'll need:

- ✓ Acrylic modeling paint (colors of your choosing)
- ✓ Toothbrush
- ✓ Dull knife

What to do:

1. Remove the ball bearings from the plastic base of the fidget spinner. Pop off the finger pads on each side, then push out each bearing. This way you won't get paint on the bearings.

2. Place the spinner down on a table covered with newspaper or plastic (or place it on a stand so that you can do this on both sides).

3. Dip the tips of the bristles of the toothbrush into the paint.

You only need a little bit of paint on the tops of the bristles.

4. Turn the brush faceup, with the bristles toward the ceiling.

Aim slightly downward toward the spinner.

5. Aiming in front of the spinner, scrape the edge of the knife toward you so that the paint splatters away from you.

Scrape the top lightly and rapidly to get the best splatter effect.

6. Let it dry and repeat on the other side.

Splatter as much as you like and with as many colors as you like!

7. Once all coats are dry, replace the bearings and place the finger pads back on top of the center bearings.

TIE-DYE

Tie-dye look spinners are all the rage but they can run on the more expensive side. Instead of plunking down $20 on a rare tie-dye spinner, trick out your $5 spinner in a few easy steps.

What you'll need:

- ✓ Two or three colors of spray paint
- ✓ A rag or old T-shirt for painting
- ✓ A spinner

What to do:

1. Cut up the rag into pieces—more pieces than you have spray paint colors.
2. Bunch up one of the rag pieces so it creates a point and give it a good spray with one color.
3. Wearing rubber gloves, pick up the rag and dab it in one spot on your spinner until it has a good dose of the color.
4. Spray your second color onto a new piece of rag.
5. Dab it in a ring around the first color.
6. Create an outer ring, either in the first color or a third color.
7. Working quickly, before it dries, pick up a clean piece of rag and drag the center color outward so it blends into the first outer ring.
8. Next, drag the color from the second ring outward so it blends with the third ring.
9. Let it dry for an hour, then flip the spinner over and repeat the process on the other side.

METAL BLING

Metal spinners are usually heavier and more expensive than standard spinners, but you can give your plastic spinner a metallic or shiny coat that will make it look just as cool and work even better than a more expensive model.

What you need:

- ✓ Metallic spray paint in gold, silver, copper, glitter blast, or shimmer
- ✓ Glitter Blast clear spray sealer
- ✓ Light-colored plastic spinner

What to do:

1. Cover the entire spinner with spray paint.
2. Wait one hour for the paint to dry fully, then flip it over and spray the other side.
3. Spray the buttons in the same color.
4. Cover all surfaces with a layer of fast-drying Glitter Blast clear spray sealer to keep it shiny for longer.

SPRAY PAINT TECHNIQUES

Take your fidget spinner out for a walk at night or bring it out at your next sleepover—when your spinner glows in the dark, amazing things can happen! Glow-in-the-dark spray paint recharges in the light and can glow for four to eight hours at a time.

You can use this same technique with chalkboard spray paint, which turns your spinner into a chalkboard; glitter spray, which adds a little *bling*; or just plain spray paint in your school colors, team colors, or whatever combination you'd like.

What you'll need:

✓ Glow, chalkboard, glitter, or any color spray paint
✓ Light-colored spinner—white works best

What to do:

1. Coat the spinner completely with the spray paint. If you're using multiple colors, hold the can at an angle so you're only spraying part of the spinner at a time. Cover the entire spinner with color.
2. Let it dry for about twenty minutes, then give it a second coat and let it dry for about an hour.
3. Flip the spinner over and repeat with the second side.

TATTOO SPINNER

Create polka dots, stripes, spots, your initials, or a tattoo to completely personalize your spinner using masking tape or shaped stickers.

What you'll need:

- ✓ Masking tape or small stickers in cool shapes like letters or animals
- ✓ Light-colored spinner
- ✓ Spray paint in one or more colors

What to do:

1. Place pieces of masking tape or stickers on both sides of the spinner where you don't want your second color to go.
2. Completely cover the spinner in spray paint and let dry for one hour.
3. Flip the spinner over and cover the second side of the spinner with paint. Let it dry for another hour.
4. Remove the stickers or tape and pop the bearings and caps back on.

HYDRO-DIPPING

To get a true tie-dye look, dip your spinner in a bucket of warm water that has spray paint floating on top.

What you'll need:

- ✓ White fidget spinner
- ✓ Large bucket (will get paint on it, so use one you don't care about)
- ✓ Two or three cans of spray paint (colors of your choosing)
- ✓ Rubber gloves
- ✓ Face mask
- ✓ Piece of cardboard for testing
- ✓ Three feet of string or thin rope

There's no spinner in the world quite like your hydro-dipped spinner!

To get started, remove the metal pieces from the spinner so that you're just working with the plastic spinner. Wipe off any dirt or grime that may be on the spinner from use.

Fact: Oil and water don't mix, so the oil-based spray paint sits on top of the water and clings to whatever you put into it, like cardboard or a plastic spinner.

What to do:

1. Fill the bucket with warm water.
2. Place the string or rope over a tree branch and let the ends hang down evenly. You'll use this line to dry

> **Tip:** You can test how the colors will look by following these same steps but using a small piece of cardboard instead of a spinner. This will show you the funky design that will come from the paint.

your spinner once it's been dipped. Use a separate line for each spinner you dip.

3. Shake the spray cans before using, then spray the paint directly into the water. You can spray both cans at once, or one at time.
4. With gloved hands, place one of your fingers (whichever fits) in the hole of the spinner. Make sure the fit is snug so that the spinner doesn't fall off while you're dipping.

5. Dip the spinner into the bucket for a few seconds. Watch how the oil stays at the surface of the water. Cooler water will make the paint filmy at the top.

6. Remove the spinner from the bucket and thread the string through the center bearing hole, then tie

the ends together. Let the spinner hang there and air dry for one hour. Do not place the wet spinner on a flat surface or it will smear your design.

7. Once the paint is dry, replace the bearings and place the finger pads back on top of the center bearings. You may need to scrape the paint off of the inside holes to pop the bearings back in.

Tip: To get the paint out of the bucket (for multiple uses), just clear the paint with a stick, dowel, or gloved hand. The paint is oily, so it will cling easily.

If the paint gets stringy, just gently pull it off. You can even smudge the paint a little to get it to spread evenly across the spinner.

PAINT-FREE SPINNER DESIGNS

Sanding

If you're looking for a more worn or classic look, sand the surfaces of your spinner and finish it off with a contrasting button instead of the matching button it came with.

What you'll need:

- ✓ Heavy-grade sandpaper
- ✓ Paper towel
- ✓ Plastic spinner
- ✓ Button covers in a contrasting color

What to do:

1. Remove the button covers and bearings.
2. Rub the sandpaper across the entire surface of the spinner, focusing on one small circular area of the spinner at a time, then moving onto the next.
3. Once you have a nice, even dullness, rinse the spinner off and dry it completely with a paper towel. Even a little dust can get into the bearings and slow it down.
4. Pop the bearings back in and finish it off with the contrasting buttons.

Frankenspinner

What's cooler than five different out-of-the-box spinners? One spinner customized from four different spinners. Follow the steps below to make a funky monster of a spinner. See how it performs differently with the different buttons and bearings!

What you'll need:

✓ One plain vanilla tri-spinner
✓ Three different metallic spinners

What to do:

1. Unscrew the metallic buttons from the metal spinners.
2. Screw them into the spoke holes of your tri-spinner to create a whole new look.

No-paint, no-mess personalized spinner

If all these projects seem a bit too messy or too much of a time commitment, you can personalize your spinner with a paint pen.

> **Tip: You can also pop out the bearings from the other spinners and place them in the spokes and center holes.**

What you'll need:

- ✓ Light-colored spinner and dark oil-based paint pen
  or
- ✓ Dark spinner and light-colored oil-based paint pen

What to do:

1. Start with a clean, dry spinner and remove the bearings.
2. Place the spinner on top of newspapers or paper towels to keep your work area clean.
3. Shake the paint pen well to mix the paint. You should hear the metal ball rattle inside to let you know it's being mixed.
4. Draw your initials or designs on the spinner.
5. Wait about ten minutes for it to dry before putting the bearings and caps back on and giving it a spin.

Triple triple

Turn your spinner into a triple spinner. It won't perform as well as a single spinner and won't do catches or most tricks, but it looks way cool!

> **Tip: Not sure what design to create?
> A swirl looks really cool when it's spinning!**

What you'll need:

- ✓ Three spinners

What to do:

1. Pop the caps off of each spinner.
2. Pop out the center bearing halfway on each of the three spinners.
3. Sandwich them together so each spinner shares a center bearing with the one next to it.
4. Put the top cap back on and give it a spin.

Heads-up lucky penny spinner

Pennies are small and light, so they don't add or subtract much in terms of spin or speed, but they add a lot to the coolness factor. Note that this mod will make outside bearings become immobile. Do not add pennies to the center bearing.

What you'll need:

- ✓ Hot glue gun and glue
- ✓ Six pennies

What to do:

1. Add a dollop of glue to the spoke or onto the "tails" side of the penny.

Tip: If you can't use hot glue, you can use Super Glue instead.

Make a small dot so the glue doesn't overflow when you press the penny down. Press it directly onto the center of the spoke or ball bearing.

2. Repeat for all six pennies on each of the spokes. Now you have a super-shiny copper spinner!

Sharpie-tastic spinner

Sharpies and other permanent markers are easy to use and come in lots of fun colors. Trick out your spinner with designs in your favorite colors and shapes: tiny dolphins and palm trees, tiger stripes, a colorful rainbow . . . the possibilities are only limited by your imagination—and the free space on your spinner.

Sparkle-riffic spinner

For some people, nothing's ever truly personalized unless they've added their own bling to it. You can find sparkles,

Use a white spinner as your blank canvas for your very own work of art!

sequins, miniature sparkle letter stickers, and faux gems at a local craft store. Attach the gems with jewel glue (also known as embellishing glue and gem glue). Let it dry completely before giving it a spin.

A little polish

Nail polish comes in many fun and funky colors and it's easy to apply to a

Make these sparkle-riffic spinners all your own with jewels, beads, or other cool accents.

plastic spinner. If you make a mistake or get tired of the design, you can scrape it off or take it off with a non-acetone nail polish remover. Ask a parent before using polish remover, and always apply nail polish in a well-ventilated area, like outdoors or in a room with open windows.

You can also use nail stickers, which are easy to find in the nail care aisle at your local drugstore. Their tiny design is made for fingernails but perfect for a small spinner! Apply the stickers, then cover them with a layer of clear or sparkly nail polish. Let it dry completely before trying it out!

MASTER THE ART OF SHOWING OFF: VIDEO TIPS

Where's the fun of becoming a fidget spinning boss if no one's there to see it? Capture your crazy tricks, cool mods, and fiercest competitions with some video footage. Get a little screen savvy with your videos with the tips below to find the best ways to set the stage, light the scene, and film a bit of fidget spinning history with your own tools from home. If it's all right with your parents, you can even upload your fidget footage to share your skills with the world!

HOW TO CREATE THE BEST FIDGET SPINNER VIDEOS

To capture your tricks on video you'll need:
- ✓ A smartphone or video camera
- ✓ A camera operator, tripod, or phone stand
- ✓ A clean space
- ✓ Good lighting
- ✓ A video editing program

PHONE STAND OR CAMERA OPERATOR? THE GOOD AND THE BAD.

	Pros	Cons
Phone Stand	· Camera is steady so the video doesn't shake · You can practice and try as many times as you want · You can cut videos on your own time without having to wait for a friend to help	· Needs more editing afterward to cut out the starts, stops, and mistakes
Friend	· Gets cool angles · Can move around to capture the action · Can start and stop the camera as needed	· Can get shaky when the camera is hand-held · Friends can be distracting

> **Tip:** **Use a head-mounted GoPro or a drone camera to capture your video from crazy angles!**

Create a basic script to work from and always talk directly to the camera. Perform tricks from easiest to hardest, saving your coolest tricks for last.

> **Tip:** **Give your tricks more flash by rolling your wrists while the spinner is spinning before performing a trick.**

Don't be afraid to make mistakes—just keep rolling the video and you can edit them out later. It's okay to include a couple of failures to show you're learning from your mistakes and to demonstrate that even an expert like you can take a few tries to get it right!

> **Tip:** **Record more video than you'll need. Edit out the unnecessary parts later.**

Consider adding captions to your video after you've edited it to make your instructions clear and easy to follow.

Take advantage of editing features to slow down your moves to show your viewers exactly how a trick is done or speed up your moves for timed videos, like timing how long you can keep a spinner going.

> **Tip:** **When creating a video to show off your tricks, perform in an area with no distractions like an unmade bed, loud pets, or annoying little brothers.**

To edit your video, you don't have to spend a fortune—or anything at all. Use free video editing software, like iMovie on a Mac or iPhone, or a site like HitFilm Express, to clip your video, add a soundtrack or voice-over, and caption your movie to make it look professional.

FIDGET SPINNER ETIQUETTE

Your spinner may help you focus, but the movement and sound may be distracting to people around you. Here are some guidelines to help you get the most out of your spinner when you're around others.

✓ Don't toss your fidget spinner or do tricks when other people are working.

✓ If you're not using it, put it away.

✓ Don't leave it spinning and walk away. The sound and movement distract others.

✓ When you need it, use it in your lap so others don't see you playing with it.

✓ Don't spin it while someone is talking to you.

✓ Clear the space around you when you practice tricks to avoid hitting people or breaking things around you.

✓ Many spinners look alike. Tag your spinner with paint, nail polish, or any of the mods in this book to avoid a case of mistaken identity.

APPENDIX

Use these charts to keep track of your accomplishments.

Spinner charts

Keep track of your spinners here.

Record book

Write down the best tricks, who broke the record, which spinner they used, when they set the record, and what the top record is to date in this handy reference chart. Now you can let the record book show who holds the record for the longest spin, the most taps, the most switches from back to front, and the most finger hops.

SPINNER CHARTS

Spinner Name	Cost	Top Spin Time	Best Trick

Spinner Name	Cost	Top Spin Time	Best Trick

Spinner Name	Cost	Top Spin Time	Best Trick

Spinner Name	Cost	Top Spin Time	Best Trick

Spinner Name	Cost	Top Spin Time	Best Trick

Spinner Name	Cost	Top Spin Time	Best Trick

Spinner Name	Cost	Top Spin Time	Best Trick

RECORD BOOK

Trick Name	Record Holder	Spinner Nickname	Date	Record!

Trick Name	Record Holder	Spinner Nickname	Date	Record!

Trick Name	Record Holder	Spinner Nickname	Date	Record!

Trick Name	Record Holder	Spinner Nickname	Date	Record!

Trick Name	Record Holder	Spinner Nickname	Date	Record!

Trick Name	Record Holder	Spinner Nickname	Date	Record!

Trick Name	Record Holder	Spinner Nickname	Date	Record!

Trick Name	Record Holder	Spinner Nickname	Date	Record!

Trick Name	Record Holder	Spinner Nickname	Date	Record!

Trick Name	Record Holder	Spinner Nickname	Date	Record!

Trick Name	Record Holder	Spinner Nickname	Date	Record!

Trick Name	Record Holder	Spinner Nickname	Date	Record!

Trick Name	Record Holder	Spinner Nickname	Date	Record!

Trick Name	Record Holder	Spinner Nickname	Date	Record!

Trick Name	Record Holder	Spinner Nickname	Date	Record!

Trick Name	Record Holder	Spinner Nickname	Date	Record!

Trick Name	Record Holder	Spinner Nickname	Date	Record!

Trick Name	Record Holder	Spinner Nickname	Date	Record!

Trick Name	Record Holder	Spinner Nickname	Date	Record!

Trick Name	Record Holder	Spinner Nickname	Date	Record!

Trick Name	Record Holder	Spinner Nickname	Date	Record!

Trick Name	Record Holder	Spinner Nickname	Date	Record!

Trick Name	Record Holder	Spinner Nickname	Date	Record!

Trick Name	Record Holder	Spinner Nickname	Date	Record!

Trick Name	Record Holder	Spinner Nickname	Date	Record!

Trick Name	Record Holder	Spinner Nickname	Date	Record!

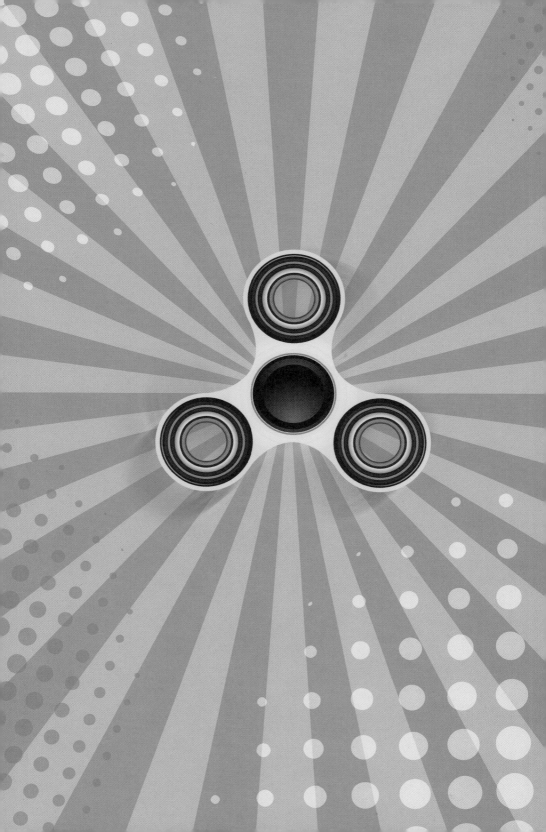